D0394790

Take
me my
bookshelves
to your arms,
And shield
me from the
cares of
life.

A Cheerful Heart

To _____

From _____

A Cheerful Heart

BY
BARBARA MILO OHRBACH

A collection of
thoughts, poems, sentiments, and recipes
to share with those you love

CLARKSON N. POTTER, INC./PUBLISHERS
NEW YORK

Grateful acknowledgment is made to the following for permission to reprint previously published material: The excerpt from *The Elder Statesman* by T. S. Eliot. Copyright © 1959 by T. S. Eliot. Renewal copyright © 1987 by Valerie Eliot. Reprinted by permission of Farrar, Straus and Giroux, Inc., and Faber and Faber Ltd. Excerpt from Sonnet XI of *Fatal Interview* by Edna St. Vincent Millay. From *Collected Poems*, Harper & Row. Copyright 1931, © 1958 by Edna St. Vincent Millay and Norma Millay Ellis. Reprinted by permission of Elizabeth Barnett, Literary Executor. The lines from "be of love (a little)" are reprinted from *No Thanks* by E. E. Cummings, edited by George James Firmage, and from *Collected Poems 1913–1962*, by permission of Liveright Publishing Corporation and William Collins, now Harper Collins Publishers, Ltd. Copyright 1935 by E. E. Cummings. Copyright © 1968 by Marion Morehouse Cummings. Copyright © 1973, 1978 by the Trustees for the E. E. Cummings Trust. Copyright © 1973, 1978 by George James Firmage. The excerpt by Hilaire Belloc is reprinted by permission of the Peters Fraser & Dunlop Group Ltd. The excerpt by John Masefield is reprinted by permission of the Society of Authors, who is the literary representative of the Estate of John Masefield. Every effort has been made to locate the copyright holders of materials used in this book. Should there be any omissions or errors, we apologize and shall be pleased to make the appropriate acknowledgments in future editions.

Published by Clarkson Potter/Publishers, 201 East 50th Street, New York, New York 10022. Member of the Crown Publishing Group.
CLARKSON N. POTTER, POTTER and colophon are trademarks of Clarkson N. Potter, Inc.

Manufactured in Japan

Design by Justine Strasberg
Endpapers by Rita Singer
Library of Congress Cataloging-in-Publication Data
A cheerful heart: a collection of thoughts, poems, sentiments, and recipes to share with those you love/[compiled] by Barbara Milo Ohrbach.—1st ed.
1. Cookery.   2. Love—Quotations, maxims, etc.
I. Ohrbach, Barbara Milo.
TX652.C487   1991
641.5—dc20   90-22953
ISBN 0-517-58181-7

10   9   8   7   6   5   4   3   2

First Edition

Recipes

F*or*
dear
Freddy and Richard

E veryone who helped on this little book
already had a cheerful heart when they started
—which is why I am so fortunate!

A big thank you to Beth Allen ♥ The folks
at Clarkson N. Potter ♥ Roy Finamore ♥
Lisa Fresne ♥ Deborah Geltman ♥ Norma
Sams ♥ Gloria Schaaf ♥ Mel, Rita, and
Harry ♥ Especially Justine Strasberg ♥ All
the people who wrote all the lovely things
about love quoted here.

Introduction

Our affections are our life. We live by them; they supply our warmth.

WILLIAM ELLERY CHANNING

As we were growing up, my mother—who loved everyone she met—was fond of quoting one of these little proverbs whenever the occasion presented itself. A favorite, "Every cloud has a silver lining," reflected her keen belief that we should all look on the bright side and for the best in people. Our family teased her about being a Pollyanna, but as time passed we realized how wise she really was. She always said, "Look for the good and you'll always find it."

A Cheerful Heart is a book my mother would like. I have tried to fill it with thoughts about the positiveness of love and caring about one another—not just women and men, but parents, children, sisters, brothers, friends, and one

generation to another. And as we all like to share special things with those we love, I have included a collection of easy and happily sweet recipes for you to make.

Montaigne said "The journey, not the arrival matters." If we look at life through human relationships, instead of all the other things that seem to get in the way, we discover how important and enduring these links are.

How nice it would be if we could continually enrich ourselves and each other by strengthening, in simple ways, the bonds between us. A thoughtful note, an unexpected visit, a big hug—it is these little, loving things that make each day worthwhile. In the long run, they support and sustain—enabling us to smile through it all. This quote by W.H. Auden says it nicely: "Among those whom I like, I can find no common denominator, but among those whom I love, I can; all of them make me laugh."

I hope you enjoy sharing this book with someone who makes *you* laugh.

Barbara Milo Ohrbach
New York City

Little drops of water,
Little grains of sand,
Make the mighty ocean
And the pleasant land.

Little deeds of kindness,
Little words of love,
Make our World an Eden
Like the heaven above.

JULIA A.
FLETCHER
CARNEY

A merry heart maketh a cheerful countenance.

PROVERB

1

This done, he took the
bride about the neck,
And kiss'd her lips with
such a clamorous smack,
That, at the parting, all
the church did echo.

SHAKESPEARE

Passion Punch Cocktails

This punch is fragrantly delicious and would be a festive addition to any wedding or other joyous occasion.

3 LARGE RIPE PEACHES
3 LARGE LEMONS
3 LARGE ORANGES
1 CUP SUGAR
3 CUPS STRAWBERRIES

3 CUPS RASPBERRIES
1 TWO-LITER BOTTLE OF GINGER ALE, CHILLED
1 QUART ICE CUBES
20 PERFECT STRAWBERRIES

✦ Blanch the peaches, remove the skins and pits, then cut them into thin slices.

✦ Peel and section the lemons and oranges.

✦ Place peaches, lemons, oranges, and sugar in a blender and process until smooth. Pour into a 6-quart punch bowl.

✦ Hull the 3 cups of strawberries and cut into halves into the blender. Add the raspberries to the blender. Process until smooth and pour into punch bowl. Stir to blend.

✦ Stir in ginger ale and ice cubes.

✦ Place a whole strawberry into each glass and ladle in the punch.

MAKES 4 QUARTS,
OR ENOUGH FOR 20 GUESTS

There is no instinct like that of the heart.

LORD BYRON

The same heart beats in every human breast.

MATTHEW ARNOLD

I will wear my heart upon my sleeve.

WILLIAM SHAKESPEARE

A loving heart is the truest wisdom.

CHARLES DICKENS

Cupid "the little greatest god."

ROBERT SOUTHEY

The heart can do anything.

I have a heart with room for every joy.

P. J. BAILEY

Love is the May-day of the heart.

BENJAMIN DISRAELI

I am alone with the beating of my heart.

LUI CHI

Love is a hole in the heart.

BEN HECHT

Love
cannot be forced,
love cannot be
coaxed and teased.
It comes out of
Heaven, unasked
and unsought.

PEARL S. BUCK

Heavenly Chocolate Mousse

So many of us are madly in love with chocolate and, believe me, this is truly the heavenliest of all my chocolate concoctions.

8 OUNCES SEMI-SWEET
  CHOCOLATE
2 TABLESPOONS
  STRONG COFFEE
2 TABLESPOONS GRAND
  MARNIER

1 EGG YOLK
2 EGG WHITES
  PINCH OF SALT
2 TABLESPOONS SUGAR
½ CUP HEAVY CREAM

✦ Melt the chocolate and coffee over low heat.

✦ Remove from the heat. Immediately add the Grand Marnier, then the egg yolk, stirring until smooth.

✦ In a large bowl, beat the egg whites and salt until soft peaks form.

✦ Add the sugar, beating until stiff peaks form.

✦ Whip the cream until stiff and fold into the egg whites. Then fold into the chocolate mixture.

✦ Chill until ready to serve. It's extra special when topped with whipped cream.

MAKES 2 HEAVENLY SERVINGS—
WITH SOME LEFT OVER FOR LATER

Love conquers all.

VIRGIL

Man can live his truth, his deepest truth, but he cannot speak it. It is for this reason that love becomes the ultimate human answer to the ultimate human question.

ARCHIBALD MACLEISH

There is no more lovely, friendly and charming relationship, communion or company than a good marriage.

MARTIN LUTHER

Love does not consist in gazing at each other but in looking outward together in the same direction.

ANTOINE DE SAINT-EXUPERY

In our life there is a single color, as on an artist's palette, which provides the meaning of life and art. It is the color of love.

MARC CHAGALL

Love is the emblem of eternity: it confounds all notion of time: effaces all memory of a beginning, all fear of an end.

MADAME DE STAEL

Madame Forestier murmured in accents of indifference: "There is no happiness comparable to that of the first hand-clasp, when the one asks: 'Do you love me?' and the other replies, 'Yes.'"

GUY DE MAUPASSANT

Come live with me,
and be my Love;
And we will all the
pleasures prove.

CHRISTOPHER MARLOWE

No sky is heavy
if the heart be light.
CHARLES CHURCHILL

Divine Angel Cake

This cake would be perfect to serve for a special gathering, when all the people you love are together. The strawberries and cream make it taste out of this world.

1¼ CUPS EGG WHITES (ABOUT 12)
1½ TEASPOONS CREAM OF TARTAR
PINCH OF SALT
1 TABLESPOON VANILLA
1 TEASPOON ALMOND EXTRACT
1½ CUPS SUGAR
1 CUP SIFTED CAKE FLOUR
2 CUPS HEAVY CREAM
3 PINTS STRAWBERRIES

✦ Preheat oven to 375°F.

✦ Using an electric mixer, beat egg whites with the cream of tartar, salt, vanilla, and almond extract until soft peaks form.

✦ Gradually add the sugar, beating until stiff.

✦ Fold flour gently into egg whites.

✦ Spoon into an ungreased 9- or 10-inch tube pan. Bake about 45 minutes. Completely cool the cake upside down, while still in the pan.

✦ Whip the cream and slice the strawberries. Slice the cake into 3 layers, then spread the cream and the berries between each layer.

MAKES 12 OR MORE DIVINE SERVINGS

11

Old books, old wine, old Nankin blue,
All things, in short, to which belong
The charm, the grace that Time makes strong—
All these I prize, but (entre nous)
Old friends are best!

AUSTIN DOBSON

Life is to be fortified by many friendships. To
love and be loved is the greatest happiness of
existence.

SYDNEY SMITH

FORGET ME NOT.

A companion loves some agreeable qualities
which a man may possess but a friend loves the
man himself.

JAMES BOSWELL

*Friendship consists in forgetting what one gives
and remembering what one receives.*

ALEXANDRE DUMAS THE YOUNGER

*How I should love to walk with you in the streets
of Blois, which must be a charming frame for
your beauty. It is an old frame, a Renaissance
frame. But it is a new frame, too, since I have
never seen you in it. And in new places the
people we love appear to us somehow new, too.*

MARCEL PROUST

*So long as we love we serve; so long as we are
loved by others I would almost say that we are
indispensable; and no man is useless while he
has a friend.*

ROBERT LOUIS STEVENSON

13

Drink to me only
with thine eyes,
And I will pledge
with mine;
Or leave a kiss but
in the cup
And I'll not look
for wine.

BEN JONSON

Pink Champagne Loving Cup

Having several dear old friends over to celebrate a happy occasion, like an anniversary, recalls the happy times you've spent together. You can use any champagne you prefer for this festive drink.

1 BOTTLE PINK CHAMPAGNE	¼ CUP COGNAC
¼ CUP SAUTERNES OR OTHER DESSERT WINE	2 LUMPS SUGAR
	1 CUP PERFECT STRAWBERRIES

✦ Chill champagne overnight.

✦ In a silver pitcher or a loving cup, mix Sauternes and cognac with sugar. Wash and add strawberries. Chill 1 hour.

✦ Pour in champagne slowly.

MAKES 4 TO 6 SERVINGS

When one has once fully entered the realm of love, the world—no matter how imperfect—becomes rich and beautiful, for it consists solely of opportunities for love.

SØREN KIERKEGAARD

It is as healthy to enjoy sentiment as to enjoy jam.

G. K. CHESTERTON

One word
Frees us of all the weight and pain of life;
That word is love.

SOPHOCLES

We loved with a love that was more than love.

EDGAR ALLAN POE

I *want to love first, and live incidentally.*

T*alk not of wasted affection; affection never was wasted.*

HENRY WADSWORTH LONGFELLOW

L*ove all love of other sights controls,*
And makes one little room an everywhere.

JOHN DONNE

G*row old along with me!*
The best is yet to be.
ROBERT BROWNING

T*wo human loves make one divine.*
ELIZABETH BARRETT BROWNING

But the beating of
my own heart
Was all the sound
I heard.

R. M. MILNES

Strawberry Flip

Almost everyone loves strawberries. This drink is a particularly nice summertime treat, when the berries are plentiful and everybody wants something easy and refreshingly cool.

1 CUP STRAWBERRIES
1 CUP MILK
½ CUP ICE CUBES

2 TEASPOONS SUGAR
2 SPRIGS FRESH MINT

- Hull the strawberries and cut into halves.
- Place all the ingredients except the mint in a blender.
- Process until smooth.
- Pour into tall, chilled glasses.
- Top with sprigs of mint.

MAKES 2 SERVINGS

W*e never know the love of our parents for us till we have become parents.*

HENRY WARD BEECHER

T*he hand that rocks the cradle
Is the hand that rules the world.*

WILLIAM ROSS WALLACE

I*t is the child in us who loves.*

ANNE MORROW LINDBERGH

T*he child alone is the true democrat; to him only is every one he meets a friend.*

ANONYMOUS

When a man is in love with one woman in a family, it is astonishing how fond he becomes of every person connected with it.

WILLIAM M. THACKERAY

There's no vocabulary
For love within a family, love that's lived in
But not looked at, love within the light of which
All else is seen, the love within which
All other love finds speech.
This love is silent.

T. S. ELIOT

Loving a child doesn't mean giving in to all his whims; to love him is to bring out the best in him, to teach him to love what is difficult.

NADIA BOULANGER

No fame, were the best less brittle,
    No praise, were it wide as earth,
Is worth so much as a little
    Child's love may be worth.

ALGERNON SWINBURNE

Under the magnetism
of friendship
the modest man
becomes bold;
the shy, confident.

WILLIAM M. THACKERAY

22

Blushing Apples

"An apple a day keeps the doctor away." And as my dear nieces and nephews will tell you, I really do believe this old saying. This recipe provides them with a welcome change, after munching fresh apples day after day.

2 ROME BEAUTY OR OTHER RED BAKING APPLES
¼ CUP BUTTER
2 TABLESPOONS FLOUR

1 TEASPOON CINNAMON
½ CUP FIRMLY PACKED DARK BROWN SUGAR
¼ CUP CHOPPED PECANS

✦ Preheat the oven to 425°F.

✦ Core the apples and peel halfway down.

✦ Place apples in a baking dish, with the peeled side up.

✦ Melt the butter, then stir in the flour, cinnamon, and brown sugar.

✦ Spoon the mixture onto the tops and into the centers of the apples. Sprinkle with pecans.

✦ Bake about 10 minutes until crusty, then lower the heat to 350°F. Bake 30 minutes until tender.

MAKES 2 SERVINGS

But there's nothing half so sweet in life
As love's young dream.

THOMAS MOORE

Love
and a cough
cannot be hid.
GEORGE
HERBERT

Ah me! love cannot be cured by herbs.

OVID

Love in the open hand, no thing but that,
Ungemmed, unhidden, wishing not to hurt,
As one should bring you cowslips in a hat
Swung from the hand, or apples in her skirt,
I bring you, calling out as children do:
"Look what I have!—And these are all for you."

EDNA ST. VINCENT MILLAY

Speak low if you speak love.
WILLIAM SHAKESPEARE

They gave each
other a smile with a
future in it.
RING LARDNER

Husband and wife come to look alike at last.
OLIVER WENDELL HOLMES

Let there be spaces in
your Togetherness.
KAHLIL GIBRAN

Love is love's reward.
JOHN DRYDEN

The greatest happiness of life is the conviction
that we are loved, loved for ourselves, or rather
loved in spite of ourselves.

VICTOR HUGO

A happy
marriage has in it
all the pleasures of
friendship, all the
enjoyments of sense
and reason, and,
indeed, all the sweets
of life.

JOSEPH ADDISON

26

Marshmallow Ambrosia

Indeed, all the sweets of life are in this ambrosia, which will please husbands and lovers, children and friends alike.

1 SMALL PINEAPPLE
2 CUPS MINIATURE MARSHMALLOWS
1 CUP FLAKED COCONUT
1 TABLESPOON LEMON JUICE
½ CUP HEAVY CREAM
2 TABLESPOONS SUGAR

✦ Cut the pineapple, removing the skin, eyes, and core. Cut into bite-size pieces and place in a serving bowl.

✦ Stir in the marshmallows and refrigerate for 2 hours.

✦ Just before serving, stir the coconut and the lemon juice into the pineapple mixture.

✦ Whip the cream until thick, add the sugar, and continue beating until stiff. Fold gently into the pineapple mixture and serve.

MAKES 4 DELICIOUS DESSERTS

Knit your hearts with an unslipping knot.

WILLIAM SHAKESPEARE

My wife is, in the strictest sense, my sole companion, and I need no other. There is no vacancy in my mind any more than in my heart.

NATHANIEL HAWTHORNE

It is only with the heart that one can see rightly; what is essential is invisible to the eye.

ANTOINE DE SAINT-EXUPERY

Mind is the partial side of man; the heart is everything.

ANTOINE DE RIVAROL

Love is never lost. If not reciprocated it will flow back and soften and purify the heart.

WASHINGTON IRVING

*Open your heart and take us in,
Love—love and me.*

WILLIAM E. HENLEY

If a good face is a letter of recommendation, a good heart is a letter of credit.

BULWER

Always I have a chair for you in the smallest parlor in the world, to wit, my heart.

EMILY DICKINSON

The streamlet's
gentle side it seeks,
The silent fount,
the shaded grot;
And sweetly to the
heart it speaks,
Forget-me-not,
forget-me-not.

FITZ-GREENE
HALLECK

30

Forget-me-not Fudge Sauce

N̲o one will forget you if you make them this terrific, very rich, warm fudge sauce. Pour it over a scoop of ice cream or top a sundae with it. It's also irresistible on a slice of simple pound cake.

3 TABLESPOONS SWEET BUTTER
½ CUP SUGAR
½ CUP FIRMLY PACKED DARK BROWN SUGAR
½ CUP DUTCH-PROCESSED COCOA
½ CUP HEAVY CREAM
1 TEASPOON VANILLA

✦ Cut butter into small pieces and place in a small, heavy saucepan.

✦ Add all the other ingredients and stir constantly over medium heat until butter has melted.

✦ Reduce heat to low and continue stirring for 5 minutes. Pour into a bowl to serve.

✦ Refrigerate any leftover sauce, then reheat over low heat before serving.

MAKES 1½ CUPS FUDGE SAUCE

I *love you more than yesterday, less than tomorrow.*

EDMOND ROSTAND

B*e of love (a little) more careful than of anything.*

E. E. CUMMINGS

A*t the touch of love everyone becomes a poet.*

PLATO

L*ove finds a way.*

ENGLISH PROVERB

W*e are shaped and fashioned by what we love.*

JOHANN WOLFGANG VON GOETHE

D*elicacy is to love what grace is to beauty.*

MADAME DE MAINTENON

'Tis better to have loved and lost
Than never to have loved at all.

ALFRED, LORD TENNYSON

Love is
a beautiful dream.

WILLIAM SHARP

 I should like to call you
by all the endearing
epithets, and yet I can
find no lovelier word than
the simple word "dear."

ROBERT SCHUMANN

Our chief want in life is someone who will make
us do what we can.

RALPH WALDO EMERSON

How did the party
go in Portman Square?
I cannot tell you;
Juliet was not there.

And how did Lady
Gaster's party go?
Juliet was next me and
I do not know.

HILAIRE BELLOC

Cranberry Ice

I *like to make ices because they are easy, yet elegant to serve. This one, a ruby pink, is a delicate dessert or an unexpected surprise with chicken or turkey. You can also make it the day before you have a special guest for dinner.*

1 CAN (16 OUNCES) JELLIED CRANBERRY SAUCE
1 CUP ORANGE JUICE

1 CUP WATER
¼ TEASPOON GRATED ORANGE PEEL

✦ In a heavy saucepan, stir all the ingredients over medium heat until smooth.

✦ Pour into a one-quart container and freeze until partially frozen.

✦ Beat 1 minute, then freeze again until firm.

✦ Let stand at room temperature 5 minutes before scooping into stemmed sherbet glasses.

MAKES 2 GENEROUS SERVINGS

Kiss the place to make it well.

ANN TAYLOR

Their lips were four
red roses on a stalk,
and, in their
summer beauty,
kiss'd each other.

WILLIAM
SHAKESPEARE

A kiss from my mother made me a painter.

BENJAMIN WEST

A long, long kiss—the kiss of youth and love.

LORD BYRON

Never a lip is curved with pain
That can't be kissed into smiles again.

BRET HARTE

Kiss
and be friends.
PETER
LANGTOFT

I'll put your basket all safe in a nook;
    Your shawl I'll hang on the willow;
And we will sigh in the daisy's eye,
    And kiss on a grass green pillow.

JOHN KEATS

You must not kiss and tell.
WILLIAM CONGREVE

No, no,
the utmost share
Of my desire shall be
Only to kiss that air
That lately kissed thee.

ROBERT HERRICK

Meringue Kisses

H*ave you finally met the man of your dreams? Now find the way to his heart. These kisses are lighter than air and make an ideal Valentine's Day gift.*

2 EGG WHITES AT
  ROOM TEMPERATURE
½ CUP CONFECTIONERS'
  SUGAR

PINCH OF SALT
1 TEASPOON WHITE
  VINEGAR
1 TEASPOON VANILLA

✦ Preheat the oven to 350°F. Line a cookie sheet with ungreased parchment paper.

✦ Beat the egg whites with an electric mixer until soft peaks form.

✦ Gradually add the sugar, salt, vinegar, and vanilla, beating until very stiff and glossy.

✦ Make 3-inch teardrop or kiss shapes by dropping mounds of meringue from a spoon onto the cookie sheet. You can also use a pastry bag.

✦ Bake about 45 minutes until the kisses are very pale brown.

✦ Turn off the oven and let the meringues dry in the oven for 25 minutes. Cool on a rack.

MAKES 8 KISSES

I love those most
whom I loved first.

THOMAS
JEFFERSON

O, Romeo,
Romeo! wherefore
art thou Romeo?

WILLIAM
SHAKESPEARE

To have and to hold from this day forward, for
better, for worse, for richer, for poorer, in
sickness, and in health, to love and to cherish, till
death us do part.

BOOK OF COMMON PRAYER

There is nothing holier, in this life of ours, than
the first consciousness of love—the first fluttering
of its silken wings.

HENRY WADSWORTH LONGFELLOW

How do I love thee? Let me count the ways.

ELIZABETH BARRETT BROWNING

Love is free.
GEOFFREY
CHAUCER

My most brilliant
achievement was
my ability to be
able to persuade my
wife to marry me.
WINSTON
CHURCHILL

An archaeologist is the best husband any
woman can have: The older she gets, the more
interested he is in her.

AGATHA CHRISTIE

The first condition of human goodness is
something to love; the second, something to
reverence.

GEORGE ELIOT

All is fair in love and war.

ENGLISH PROVERB

All love is sweet,
Given or returned.
Common as light is love,
And its familiar voice
wearies not ever.

PERCY BYSSHE SHELLEY

Honeybunch Shake

I make this shake for my honeybunch, Mel, all the time. It's quick, satisfying, and filled with healthy ingredients— just the thing for mornings when there isn't enough time for a big breakfast.

1 BANANA
1 CUP MILK
1 CUP PLAIN YOGURT
1 TABLESPOON HONEY

2 TEASPOONS LEMON JUICE
1 TEASPOON FLAKED COCONUT

✦ Slice the banana into the blender.
✦ Add all the remaining ingredients except the coconut.
✦ Process until smooth and chill about 15 minutes.
✦ Pour into glasses and sprinkle with the coconut.

MAKES 2 TALL SERVINGS

With all beings and all things we shall be as relatives.

SIOUX INDIAN PROVERB

Are there any brothers who do not criticize a bit and make fun of the fiancé who is stealing a sister from them?

COLETTE

Be you, my dear, the link of love, union, and peace for the whole family. The world will give you the more credit for it, in proportion to the difficulty of the task.

THOMAS JEFFERSON

The greatest love is a mother's; then comes a dog's; then comes a sweetheart's.

POLISH PROVERB

Can a mouse fall in love with a cat?

THOMAS FULLER

God could not be everywhere, so He made mothers.

YIDDISH PROVERB

Be kindly affectioned one to another with brotherly love.

ROMANS

Other things may change us, but we start and end with the family.

ANTHONY BRANDT

When I write of
hunger, I am really
writing about love
and the hunger for it,
and warmth and
the love of it . . . and
it is all one.

M. F. K. FISHER

Sweet Potato Pie

How about making a pie of sweet potatoes, instead of the same old thing? It's a nice surprise for dessert and a lovely gift to bring with you when visiting your family and friends during the holidays.

3 EGGS
1½ CUPS EVAPORATED MILK
1 CUP FIRMLY PACKED DARK BROWN SUGAR
2 TEASPOONS CINNAMON
¼ TEASPOON GROUND CLOVES

PINCH OF SALT
1¼ CUPS COOKED AND MASHED SWEET POTATOES
1 TABLESPOON RUM OR MAPLE SYRUP
1 UNBAKED 9- OR 10-INCH PIE CRUST

+ Preheat oven to 425°F.
+ Beat the eggs and the milk in a large bowl.
+ Add the sugar, cinnamon, cloves, salt, sweet potatoes, and rum. Stir until smooth.
+ Spoon into the unbaked crust.
+ Bake 45 minutes or until filling is set.

MAKES 8 SERVINGS

Life is a flower of which
love is the honey.

VICTOR HUGO

Love is space and time
measured by the heart.

MARCEL PROUST

There is time for work. And time for love. That
leaves no other time.

COCO CHANEL

A man in the
house is worth two
in the street.

MAE WEST

I wonder, by my troth,
what thou and I
did till we loved?

JOHN DONNE

Love's like the flies, and, drawing room or garden, goes all over a house.

DOUGLAS JERROLD

Dora and I are now married, but just as happy as we were before.

BERTRAND RUSSELL

Unshared joy is an unlighted candle.

SPANISH PROVERB

For five whole years I see her every day, and always think I see her for the first time.

JEAN RACINE

A book of verses underneath the bough,
A jug of wine, a loaf of bread—and thou
    Beside me singing in the wilderness.

OMAR KHAYYAM

Lord! I wonder what
fool it was that first
invented kissing.
JONATHAN SWIFT

50

Raspberry Fool

Be sure to make this *wonderful, smooth, and fluffy dessert during the all-too-short raspberry season, especially if you have a raspberry patch. You won't fool anyone— they'll just think you are a very talented cook!*

1½ CUPS RASPBERRIES	1 CUP HEAVY CREAM
⅓ CUP SUGAR	1 TEASPOON VANILLA

✦ Wash the raspberries gently. Set 10 aside for a garnish and put the remaining berries into a bowl.

✦ Add the sugar and let stand at room temperature for 1 hour.

✦ Purée raspberries in a blender or food processor, then press through a sieve to remove the seeds.

✦ Whip the cream until stiff, adding the vanilla.

✦ Gently fold the raspberry purée into the cream.

✦ Chill at least 2 hours until cold. Serve with reserved berries on top.

MAKES 2 GENEROUS SERVINGS

A good deed is never lost; he who sows courtesy reaps friendship, and he who plants kindness gathers love.

ST. BASIL

Because in spite of everything I still believe that people are really good at heart.

ANNE FRANK

Clasp
the hands and
know the thoughts
of men in other lands.
JOHN
MASEFIELD

You and I ought not to die before We have explained ourselves to each other.

JOHN ADAMS

The ancients held, it is said, that each human being is but half of a perfect unit; and that the divine healing of life's wounds comes only when one has the rare good fortune to meet the half of himself. Then are both, as Plato writes, "smitten with a friendship in a wondrous way": and these continue to be friends through life.

J. C. DIER

Having someone wonder where you are when you don't come home at night is a very old human need.

MARGARET MEAD

Love . . . is like
a beautiful flower
which I may not
touch, but whose
fragrance makes
the garden a place
of delight just
the same.

HELEN KELLER

Fragrant Rose Petal Jam

Surprise your best friend and bring some of this jam as a hostess gift, instead of flowers, the next time you visit. A clear glass jar filled with pale pink jam and tied with a flowery ribbon is a thoughtful token.

1 CUP PINK ROSE PETALS, LIGHTLY PACKED

1 CUP SUGAR

¾ CUP WATER

2 TEASPOONS LEMON JUICE

✦ Pick the most fragrant rose petals possible. Carefully wash and dry them.

✦ In a heavy saucepan, mix the sugar, water, and lemon juice.

✦ Stir in the petals and let stand for 1 hour.

✦ Bring to a boil over medium heat, reduce heat and simmer for 20 minutes. Watching carefully, stir gently and frequently until jam begins to thicken.

✦ Cool. Serve with hot scones or biscuits. Store any extra jam in a covered jar. Can be kept in the refrigerator for about a week.

MAKES 1 CUP JAM

Love comforteth like sunshine after rain.
WILLIAM SHAKESPEARE

A Pledge of constant Love from one

Sincerely attached!

Time is
Too slow for those who wait,
Too swift for those who fear,
Too long for those who grieve,
Too short for those who rejoice,
But for those who love, time is
Eternity. Hours fly, flowers die,
new days, new ways, pass by.
Love stays.
SUNDIAL INSCRIPTION

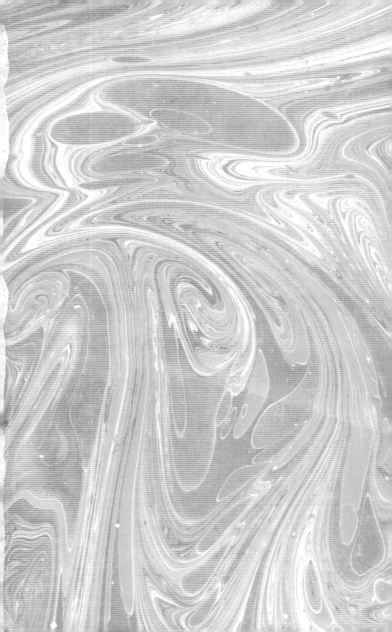

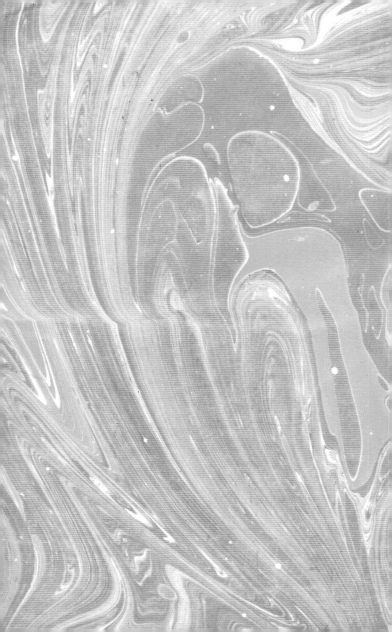